Patron Saints
A COMPLETE REFERENCE GUIDE

Edited by
Diarmuid Clifford, O.P.

Illustrated by
William Luberoff
and
Robert Berran

Regina
Press

Nihil Obstat: Reverend Robert O. Morrisey, J.C.D.
                 Censor librorum
                 August 8th, 2002

Imprimatur: Most Reverend William Murphy
                 Bishop of Rockville Centre
                 September 12, 2002

THE REGINA PRESS
10 Hub Drive
Melville, New York 11747

All rights reserved. No part of this publication may be reproduced or transmitted in any form or by any means, electronic or mechanical, including photocopying, recording, or any information storage and retrieval system, without permission in writing from the publishers.

Published by Regina Press under arrangement
with St. Martin Apostolate, Dublin, Ireland.

If any required credits have been omitted, it is unintentional, and the publisher will correct any omisions in future reprints.

© Copyright 2002, 2005 by The Regina Press
Artwork © 2002, 2005 Reproducta, NY

ISBN 0-88271-125-3

Printed in Hong Kong.

Table of Contents

Introduction

*F*rom the time of the Apostles up to the 21st century the Church has been blessed with saints, Christians renowned for their holiness. People, recognizing that they had lead holy lives and were now in God's presence, began asking their help. We ask saints to pray for us because we believe their prayers can help us. Their prayers for us are more powerful than the prayers of anyone here on earth because they are close to God. It is only natural then that we ask their help for anything important to us.

Because they came to be regarded as being particularly helpful in certain areas of life or with regard to special needs, some saints became known as Patron saints. Over the years patron saints became more numerous, and ranged from being patrons of countries or places in the early years, to, in later years, becoming patrons of practically every kind of human activity, work or need. In modern times a patron saint is usually designated so by the Church. In earlier days, the selection was prompted by popular choice. This book gives a concise list of the many saints whose lives have influenced successive generations. Who are the Saints and the reasons why many of these became patron saints is explained in the opening article.

Robert Berran. *St. Patrick (Contemporary)*

Who are the Saints?

*S*aints are the heroes of the Christian Church. They are Christians remembered for their great holiness and show us what holiness really means. Some saints were revered as holy people during their lifetimes. The praise they received while living continues on after their deaths. Stories of their lives were passed on to children, grandchildren and successive generations and have inspired the Church ever since their deaths.

The Church looks on the saints as people with a message for all Christians. They tell us that with the help of God we can all be saints; that the Spirit of Christ working in us can overcome weakness and sinfulness and lead us to holiness and closer union with God.

Because the saints show us what holiness means, the Church sees them as models for us to imitate. This does not mean that we should pick a saint and live exactly like that saint. The church presents them as examples of how our lives should be guided and inspired by a love of God. They serve as models for us because they were weak and sinners like us. They have shown us what ordinary human beings like us can achieve when we make God an important part of our lives, when we try with God's help to do what God asks of us. Each saint is unique. No two saints are exactly alike. This reminds us that we too are unique and that in trying to be holy we should be ourselves.

The presence of the saints in heaven reminds us that heaven is also our future home. We too can look forward to a life of eternal happiness with God. Their victory over sin and all obstacles to their eternal salvation encourages us to continue our struggle against sin with the joyous hope of one day seeing God face to face. We praise, honor and learn from the saints and also look forward to joining them in our heavenly home.

From the earliest times of the Church, people have always prayed to the saints and asked the saints to intercede for them — to put in a word for them with God. Just as here on earth we pray for one another, so we can also ask the saints to pray for us. They are in God's presence, nearer to God than our friends and neighbors here on earth. It is only natural that we ask their help for anything important to us. Their prayers for us are more powerful than the prayers of anyone here on earth because they are already in the presence of God.

Patron Saints

*H*aving died and being in the glory of God, the saints are free from limits of time and space. By prayer we can ask for their aid at any time or in any place. When they were alive, they lived — and died — in a certain place where they are best remembered. The place where they were buried became connected to their memory and their tombs became shrines and places of pilgrimage. An example is found in the words written on the tomb of St. Martin of Tours: "Here lies Martin the bishop, of holy memory, whose soul is in the hand of God; but he is fully here, present and made plain by every kind of favor." Martin became Patron Saint of the place where he was buried, just as many others became patron saints of the region and places where their tombs were located. The martyrs are the earliest example of local patrons. The date of the martyr's death became celebrated like his or her birthday - their birthday into Heaven. Later, saints were venerated who were not martyrs. St. Martin of Tours, who died near the year 400, was one of these. Saints like Martin were known for their holiness and for their power of intercession with God. For the first thousand years of Christianity, most of these saints lived in monasteries and they became patrons of the local area.

After the year 1000 the patronage of saints extended to the work people were doing, their occupations, their professions and specific needs. The choice of the patron was usually linked to something in the life of the saint. For example, the martyrs Cosmas and Damian were patron saints of physicians, because they were known as doctors. They also were patron saints of barbers, because doctors back then were also known as barbers. St. Martin de Porres, who had some medical training in medicine was also a barber and joins Cosmas and Damian as a patron of barbers.

Some saints are asked for help when people have specific troubles. Usually the saint had had the same problem and could understand the need. One old source book that helped in choosing early patrons was called *The Golden Legend* by James of Voragine. James wrote his book near the year 1300. He wrote about St. Blaise: "A woman brought to him her son, who had a fishbone caught in his throat; and setting him down at the hermit's feet, tearfully besought him to heal the child. And St. Blaise, extending his hands over him, prayed God to cure him; and instantly the child was made well." St. Blaise is the patron of sore throats and people still come to have their throats blessed on his feast day.

Diarmuid Clifford OP

Principal Patronages of Saints

Abandoned People
  Flora

Accountants
  Matthew

Actors
  Genesius

Advertisers
  Bernardine of Siena

Advocates
  Ives

African Americans
  Charles Lwanga
    and Companions
  Martin de Porres

Agricultural Workers
  Phocas
  Walstan

Alcoholics
  John of God
  Matthew
  Monica

Alpinists
  Bernard of Montjoux

Altar Servers
  John Berchmans

Ammunition Workers
  Barbara

Amputees
  Anthony

Robert Berran. *St. Monica and Augustine (Contemporary)*

Anesthetists
  Rene Goupil

Anglers
  Andrew

Animals and Birds
  Francis of Assisi

Animals, Domestic
  Anthony of Egypt

Animal Welfare Society
  Francis of Assisi

Apostleship of Prayer
  Francis Xavier

Apple Orchards
  Charles Borromeo

Apprentices
  John Bosco

Archaeologists
  Damasus
  Helen
  Jerome

Archers
  George
  Sebastian

Architects
  Barbara
  Thomas the Apostle

Armorers
  Dunstan

Arthritis Sufferers
  James the Greater

Artists
  Catherine of Bologna
  Fra Angelico
  Luke

Robert Berran. *St. Francis (Contemporary)*

Astronauts
Joseph of Cupertino

Astronomers
Dominic

Athletes
Sebastian

Automobiles
Christopher

Aviators and Air Passengers
Joseph of Cupertino

Our Lady of Loreto

Therese of Lisieux

Bachelors
Casimir of Poland

Christopher

Roch

Bakers
Elizabeth of Hungary

Nicholas of Myra

Bankers
Matthew

Barbers
Cosmas and Damian

Martin de Porres

Basket Weavers
Anthony of Egypt

Battle
Michael

Bee Keepers
Ambrose

Beggars
Martin of Tours

Bishops
Ambrose
Charles Borromeo

Blind People
Lawrence
Lucy
Odilia
Raphael
Thomas the Apostle

Blood Banks
Januarius
John the Apostle

Boatmen
John Roche
Julian the Hospitaler

Bodily Ills
Our Lady of Lourdes

Bookkeepers
Matthew

Booksellers
John of God
John the Apostle

Boys
Aloysius Gonzaga
Dominic Savio
John Berchmans
John Bosco
Nicholas of Myra

Boy Scouts
George

Brass Workers
Barbara

Brewers
Augustine of Hippo
Luke
Nicholas of Myra

Bricklayers
Stephen

Brides
Nicholas of Myra

Bridge Builders
John of Nepomucene

Peter

Broadcasters
Gabriel

Builders
Barbara

Vincent Ferrer

Bus Drivers
Christopher

Businesswomen
Margaret of York

Butchers
Anthony of Egypt

Cabinet Makers
Anne

Cancer Patients
Peregrine

Candle Makers
Ambrose

**Canonists
(Canon Lawyers)**
Raymond of Penafort

Carpenters
Joseph

Matthias

Thomas the Apostle

Carvers
Olaf

Casket Makers
Stephen

Robert Berran. *St. Peregrine (Contemporary)*

Catechists
Charles Borromeo
Robert Bellarmine
Viator

Catholic Action
Francis of Assisi

Catholic Charities
Elizabeth of Hungary

Catholic Education
John Neumann
Joseph Calasanz

Catholic Press
Francis de Sales

Catholic Universities
Thomas Aquinas

Cattle Diseases
Sebastian

Cavalry
George

Cemeteries
Anne

Charitable Societies
Elizabeth of Hungary
Vincent de Paul

Chastity
Thomas Aquinas

Chemical Industries
Cosmas and Damian

Childbirth
Claire of Assisi
Gerard Majella

Children
Lambert
Nicholas of Myra

Robert Berran. *St. George (Contemporary)*

Children, Adopted
  Thomas More

  William

Children, Convulsive
  Scholastica

Children, Sick
  Bueno

Chivalry
  George

Christian Unity
  Cyril and Methodius

Choirboys
  Dominic Savio

  Holy Innocents

Church, The
  Joseph

  Peter

Church Sextons
  Theobald

Civil Servants
  Thomas More

Clothworkers
  Homobonus

Clock Makers
  Peter

Coachmen
  Richard of Chicester

Coin Collectors
  Eligius (Eloi)

Colic Sufferers
  Charles Borromeo

Comedians
  Genesius

  Vitus

Communications Personnel
Bernardine of Siena

Composers
Cecilia

Compositors
John the Apostle

Confectioners
Cosmas and Damian

Confessors
Alphonsus Liguori

Francis de Sales

John of Nepomucene

John Vianney

Construction Workers
Thomas the Apostle

Converts
Jason

Cooks
Lawrence

Martha

Coppersmiths
Maurus

Councilmen
Nicholas of Flue

Counsel
Holy Spirit

Countesses
Elizabeth of Hungary

Counts
Charles the Good

Gerald of Aurillac

Court Workers
Thomas More

Cows
Perpetua

Crippled People
Gilbert of Sempringham
Giles

Crusaders
Charles the Good
Louis IX

Cursillo
Paul

Cutters
Lucy

Dairy Workers
Bridget of Ireland

Dancers
Genesius
Philemon
Vitus

Deacons
Lawrence
Marinus
Stephen

Deaf People
Francis de Sales

Death and Dying
Benedict
Margaret of Scotland

Death, Happy
Joseph

Death of Children
Elizabeth of Hungary
Felicity
Stephen

Death, Solitary
Francis of Assisi

William Luberoff. *St. Joseph (Contemporary)*

Death, Sudden
  Barbara

Dentists
  Apollonia
  Cosmas and Damian

Desperate Cases
  Gregory of Neocaesarea
  Jude Thaddeus
  Rita of Cascia

Dieticians
  Martha

Diplomats
  Gabriel

Disabled People
  Alphais
  Gerald of Aurillac
  Henry II
  Seraphina
  Servulus

Divorced
  Fabiola
  Guntramnus
  Helena

Dogs
  Hubert

Dog Bite Victims
  Hubert
  Vitus

Dog Lovers
  Roch

Domestic Abuse Victims
  Fabiola
  Godaleva
  Margaret the Barefooted
  Monica
  Pharaildis

Domestic Workers
  Martha

Dominicans
Dominic

Doubters
Joseph

Drug Addicts
Maximilian Kolbe

Duchesses
Hedwig
Ludmila

Dukes
Henry II

Dyers
Lydia
Maurice

Earache Sufferers
Polycarp

Ecologists
Francis of Assisi

Ecumenists
Cyril and Methodius
Josaphat

Editors
John Bosco

Embroiderers
Claire of Assisi

Emigrants
Frances Xavier Cabrini

Empresses
Adelaide
Helen

Engineers
Ferdinand of Castile
Joseph

Enemies of Religion
Sebastian

Engravers
John the Apostle

Enlightenment
Our Lady of Good
Counsel

Epilepsy, Motor Diseases
Dymphna

Genesius

Vitus

Willibrord

Eucharistic Congresses and Societies
Paschal Baylon

Eyes and Eye Diseases
Claire of Assisi

Lucy

Raphael

Faith in Blessed Sacrament
Anthony

Falsely Accused
Dominic Savio

Raymond Nonnatus

Families
Joseph

Families of Addicts
Maximilian Kolbe

Family Harmony
Dymphna

Farmers
George

Isidore the Farmer

Farm Workers
Benedict

Fathers
Joseph

Robert Berran. *St. Dympna (Contemporary)*

Fear of the Lord
Holy Spirit

Fieldworkers
Notburga

Fever Patients
Genevieve

Peter

Firefighters
Agatha

Florian

Lawrence

Fire Prevention
Catherine of Siena

Fire
Francis of Assisi

Lawrence

Fireworks
Barbara

First Communicants
Tarcisius

Fishermen
Andrew

Nicholas of Myra

Peter

Fishmarkets
Magnus

Florists
Dorothy

Rose of Lima

Therese of Lisieux

Foreign Missions
Benedict the Black

Francis Xavier

Peter Claver

Therese of Lisieux

Forest Workers
John Gualbert

Foundlings
Holy Innocents

Foot Trouble
Peter

Fortifications
Barbara

Fortitude
Holy Spirit

Founders
Barbara

Frenzy
Peter

Funeral Directors
Dismas
Joseph of Arimathea
Sebastian

Gardeners
Adelard
Dorothy

Fiacre
Rose of Lima
Sebastian

Girls
Agnes
Maria Goretti

Glaziers
Luke
Mark

Goldsmiths
Anastasius
Dunstan
Eligius (Eloi)
Luke

Gout Sufferers
Andrew

Governors
Ferdinand of Castile

Grandmothers
Anne

Grave Diggers
Anthony of Egypt

Greetings
Valentine

Grocers
Michael

Grooms, Young
Louis IX

Nicholas of Myra

Guardians
Guntramnus

Joseph

Gunners (Artillery)
Barbara

Hairdressers (Women's)
Mary Magdalen

Hairdressers (Men's)
Cosmas and Damian

Martin de Porres

Hardware
Sebastian

Hatters
Clement

James the Less

Headache Sufferers
Dennis

Stephen

Teresa of Avila

Heart Patients
John of God

Teresa of Avila

Robert Berran. *St. Michael (Contemporary)*

Hermits
 Anthony of Egypt

 Giles

Hesitators
 Joseph

Home Builders
 Our Lady of Loreto

Homeless People
 Benedict Labre

 Edwin

 Elizabeth of Hungary

 Lufthild

 Margaret of Cortona

Homemakers, Housekeepers
 Anne

 Martha

 Zita

Hopeless Cases
 Jude Thaddeus

Hope, Never Failing
 Our Lady of
  Perpetual Help

Horses
 Giles

 Hippolitus

Horseriders
 Anne

Hospitals
 Camillus de Lellis

 John of God

Hospital Administrators
 Basil the Great

 Frances Xavier Cabrini

Hospital Pharmacists
 Gemma Galgani

Hospital Workers
Jude Thaddeus

Vincent de Paul

Hoteliers
Amand

Martha

Hunters
Eustace

Hubert

Impenitence
Barbara

Infantrymen
Maurice

Intestinal Sufferers
Eramus

Invalids
Roch

Janitors
Theobald

Jealousy, Victims of
Elizabeth of Portugal

Hedwig of Poland

Jewelers
Dunstan

Eligius (Eloi)

Luke

Journalists
Francis de Sales

Judges
Ives

Jurists
John Capistrano

John Chrysostom

Kidnap Victims
Arthelais

Kings

Casimir of Poland

Edgar

Edmund

Edwin

Edward the Confessor

Henry

Louis IX

Olaf

Stephen of Hungary

Knights

George

James the Greater

Julian the Hospitaler

Knowledge

Holy Spirit

Laborers

Isidore the Farmer

James the Greater

John Bosco

Joseph

Lace Makers

Our Lady of Loreto

Sebastian

Lawyers

Genesius

Ives

Thomas More

Lay Apostolate

Paul

Lay Brothers

Gerard Majella

Lay Sisters

Martha

Learning

Ambrose

Robert Berran. *St. Thomas More (Contemporary)*

Leather Workers
Crispin and Crispinian

Lectors
Pollio

Sabas

Lepers
Giles

Vincent de Paul

Librarians
Jerome

Raymond of Penafort

Life, Longevity
Kevin

Peter

Lighthouse Keepers
Clement of Alexandria

Lightning
Barbara

Linguists
Gotteschalc

Lithographers
John the Apostle

Locksmiths
Dunstan

Eligius (Eloi)

Lost Articles
Anthony of Padua

Lonely People
Rita

Lovers
Raphael

Valentine

Lumbago Sufferers
Lawrence

Machinists
Hubert

Magistrates
Nicholas of Flue

Maids
Zita

Marble Workers
Clement of Rome

Mariners
Brendan

Francis of Paola

Michael

Nicholas of Myra

Star of the Sea

Marriage
Francis Regis

Marriages, Difficult
Edward the Confessor

Elizabeth of
Portugal

Fabiola

Monica

Helen

Thomas More

Marriages, Second
Adelaide

Matilda

Mathematicians
Hubert

Meetings, Happy
Raphael

Medical Technicians and Technologists
Albert the Great

Mentally Ill
Benedict Labre

Drogo

Dymphna

Merchants
Francis of Assisi
Homobonus
Nicholas of Myra

Metal Workers
Eligius (Eloi)

Messengers
Gabriel

Midwives
Margaret of Cortona
Pantaleon
Raymond Nonnatus

Military Chaplains
John Capistrano

Miners
Barbara

Missionary Priests
Vincent Pallotti

Missions, Parish
Leonard of
Port Maurice

Monks
Anthony of Egypt
Benedict
John the Baptist

Mothers
Anne
Blessed Virgin Mary
Gerard Majella
Monica
Nicholas of Tolentino

Mothers, Expectant
Gerard Majella

Mothers, Single
Margaret of Cortona

Robert Berran. *St. Gerard (Contemporary)*

Motorcyclists
Our Lady of Grace
Our Lady of the
Miraculous Medal

Motorists
Christopher
Frances of Rome

Mountaineers
Bernard of Montjoux

Murderers
Vladimir

Musicians
Cecilia
Dunstan
Gregory the Great

Mystics
John of the Cross

Navigators
Brendan
Francis of Paola
Star of the Sea

Needleworkers
Francis of Assisi

Net Makers
Peter

Notaries
Luke
Mark

Nurses
Agatha
Camillus de Lellis
Cosmas and Damian
Elizabeth of Hungary
John of God
Raphael

Nursing and Nursing Services
Elizabeth of Hungary

Catherine of Siena

Nursing Homes
Elizabeth of Hungary

Luke

Mark

Nuns
Bridget of Sweden

Scholastica

Obstetricians
Raymond Nonnatus

Opticians
Mark

Orators
John Chrysostom

Organ Builders
Cecilia

Genesius

Orphans
Frances Xavier Cabrini

Jerome Emiliani

Painters
Luke

Pall Bearers
Joseph of Arimathea

Paper Makers
John the Apostle

Paralyzed People
Osmund

Paratroopers
Michael

Parents of Large Families
Vladimir

Parish Priests
John Vianney

Pawnbrokers
Nicholas of Myra

Peasants
Lucy

Peddlers
Lucy

Pencil Makers
Thomas Aquinas

Penitents
Mary Magdalen

Perfumers
Nicholas of Myra

Pharmacists
Cosmas and Damian

James the Greater

Nicholas of Myra

Raphael

Philosophers
Justin Martyr

Physicians
Cosmas and Damian

Luke

Pantaleon

Raphael

Sebastian

Piety
Holy Spirit

Pilots
Joseph of Cupertino

Pioneers
Joseph

Pilgrims
James the Greater

Robert Berran. *St. Lucy (Contemporary)*

Plague Victims
Roch

Sebastian

Plasterers
Bartholomew

Poets
Cecilia

Plumbers
Vincent Ferrer

Poison Sufferers
Benedict

Police Officers
Michael

Poor
Anthony of Padua

Lawrence

Martin de Porres

Poor Souls
Nicholas of Tolentino

Popes
Peter

Gregory the Great

Porters
Christopher

Possessed People
Bruno

Dennis

Lucian and Marcian

Margaret of Fantana

Postal Employees
Gabriel

Potters
Goar

Sebastian

Preachers
Bernardine of Siena

John Chrysostom

Priests

Charles Borromeo

Gabriel Possenti

John of Avila

John Vianney

Vincent Pallotti

Princes

Boris and Gleb

Casimir of Poland

Gotteschalc

Princesses

Adelaide

Dymphna

Printers

Augustine of Hippo

Genesius

John of God

Prisons

Joseph Cafasso

Prisoners

Adelaide

Barbara

Louis IX

Vincent de Paul

Public Education

Martin de Porres

Public Health Services

Martin de Porres

Public Relations

Bernardine of Siena

Public Relations (Hospitals)

Paul

Publishers

Paul

John the Apostle

John Bosco

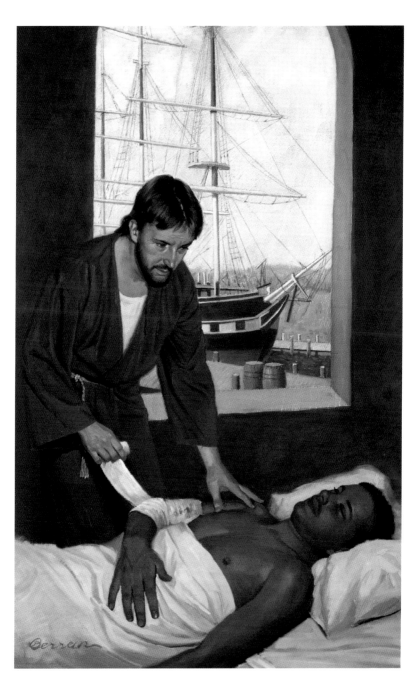

Queens
Elizabeth of Portugal

Hedwig of Poland

Margaret of Scotland

Rabies Victims
Hubert

Race Relations
Martin de Porres

Peter Claver

Racquet Makers
Sebastian

Radiologists
Michael

Radio Workers
Gabriel

Refugees
Alban

Restaurants
Martha

Retreats
Ignatius of Loyola

Rheumatism Sufferers
James the Greater

Rope Makers
Paul

Runaways
Alodia

Dymphna

Saddlers
Crispin and Crispinian

Lucy

Safe Journeys
Raphael

Robert Berran. *St. Peter Claver (Contemporary)*

Sailors
  Andrew
  Brendan
  Christopher
  Cuthbert
  Michael
  Nicholas of Myra
  Star of the Sea

Salespeople
  Lucy

Savings Banks
  Anthony Claret

Scholars
  Bede
  Bridget of Ireland
  Jerome
  Thomas Aquinas

Schools (Catholic)
  Joseph Calasanz
  Thomas Aquinas

Scientists
  Albert the Great

Sculptors
  Castorius
  Claude la Colombiere
  Luke

Secretaries
  Genesius
  Mark

Seminarians
  Charles Borromeo

Servants
  Martha
  Zita

William Luberoff. *St. Christopher (Contemporary)*

Servicewomen
Joan of Arc
Genevieve

Shepherds
Bernadette
Cuthbert
Cuthman
Drogo
Germaine Cousin
Raphael

Shoemakers
Crispin and Crispinian

Ship Builders
Peter

Sick People
Camillus de Lellis
Germaine Cousin
John of God

Louis IX
Martin de Porres
Michael

Silversmiths
Andronicus

Singers
Cecilia
Gregory the Great

Skaters
Lidwina

Skiers
Bernard of Montjoux

Skin Disease Sufferers
Peregrine

Skin Rashes
Anthony of Padua
George

William Luberoff. *St. Bernadette (Contemporary)*

Sleepwalkers
Dymphna

Smiths
Eligius (Eloi)

Snake Bite Sufferers
Patrick

Paul

Vitus

Social Justice
Martin de Porres

Joseph

Social Workers
Louise de Marillac

Soldiers
Adrian

George

Ignatius of Loyola

Joan of Arc

Martin of Tours

Sebastian

Speleologists
Benedict

Spinners
Seraphina

Spiritual Directors
Charles Borromeo

Spiritual Help
Vincent de Paul

Spouses
Joseph

Spouses, Separated
Edward the Confessor

Starving People
Anthony of Padua

Stationers
Peter

Stenographers
Cassian

Genesius

Stepparents
Leopold
Thomas More

Stockbrokers
Matthew

Stomach Trouble
Charles Borromeo

Timothy

Stone Cutters
Clement of Rome

Stone Masons
Barbara

Sebastian

Stephen

Storms
Barbara

Students
Catherine of
Alexandria

Gregory

Jerome

Joseph of Cupertino

Thomas Aquinas

Students, Theological
Albert the Great

Surgeons
Cosmas and Damian

Luke

Swans
Sebastian

Swordsmiths
Maurice

Tailors
  Homobonus

  John the Baptist

Tanners
  Bartholomew

  Crispin and Crispinian

Tax Collectors
  Matthew

Taxi Drivers
  Fiacre

Teachers
  Francis de Sales

  Gregory the Great

  John Baptist
    de la Salle

Telecommunications
  Gabriel

Television
  Claire of Assisi

  Gabriel

Temptation
  Michael

Theologians
  Alphonsus Liguori

  Augustine of Hippo

  John the Apostle

  Thomas Aquinas

Thieves, Repentant
  Dismas

Throats
  Catherine of Alexandria

Throat Ailment Sufferers
  Blaise

William Luberoff. *St. John the Baptist (Contemporary)*

Toothache Sufferers
Apollonia

Osmund

Patrick

Torture Victims
Agatha

Charles Lwanga
and Companions

Edmund

Tramps
Benedict Labre

Joseph

Travelers
Anthony of Padua

Christopher

Nicholas of Myra

Paul

Raphael

Travel
Bona

Truck Drivers
Christopher

Tuberculosis Sufferers
Therese of Lisieux

Gemma Galgani

Tumors
Rita

Ulcers
Charles Borromeo

Understanding
Holy Spirit

Unfaithfulness, Victims of
Catherine of Genoa

Elizabeth of Portugal

Fabiola

Monica

Universal Church
Joseph

William Luberoff. *St. Joseph (Contemporary)*

Universities
Thomas Aquinas

Vanity
Rose of Lima

Virgins
Blessed Virgin Mary

Vocations
Alphonsus Liguori

Vocations, Lost
Gotteschalc

Volcanic Eruptions
Januarius

Waiters
Martha

Warehouses
Barbara

Watchmen
Peter of Alcantara

Weavers
Bernardine of Siena
Maurice

Whales
Brendan

Widowers
Edgar
Thomas More

Widows
Anne
Catherine of Genoa
Elizabeth Ann Seton
Elizabeth of Hungary
Elizabeth of Portugal
Felicity
Frances of Rome
Margaret of Scotland
Matida
Monica
Paula

Berran

Wine Trade
Amand

Francis Xavier

Vincent of Saragossa

Wisdom
Holy Spirit

Wolves
Peter

Women in Labor
Anne

Women, Pregnant
Anne

Gerard Majella

Women, Single
Agatha

Andrew

Margaret of Cortona

Women, Unhappily Married
Rita of Cascia

Women, Unable to Have Children
Anne

Felicity

Workers
Bonaventure

Joseph

Wounds, Healing
Rita of Cascia

Writers
Francis de Sales

John the Apostle

Lucy

Paul

Robert Berran. *St. Anne (Contemporary)*

Yachtsmen

Adjutor

Brendan

Star of the Sea

Youth

Aloysius Gonzaga

Gabriel Possenti

John Berchmans

Patron Saints of Places and Countries

Africa

Mary, Queen of Africa

Algeria

Cyprian of Carthage

Alsace

Odilia

Americas

Our Lady
of Guadalupe

Rose of Lima

Angola

Immaculate Heart
of Mary

Argentina

Gabriel

Our Lady of Lujan

Armenia

Bartholomew

Gregory the Illuminator

Asia Minor

John the Apostle

Australia

Our Lady Help
of Christians

Austria

Colman

Florian

Joseph

Leopold III

Maurice

Bavaria

Kilian

Belgium
  Joseph
  John of Nepomucene

Bohemia
  Adalbert
  Cyril and Methodius
  John of Nepomucene
  Joseph
  Norbert
  Wenesclaus

Bolivia
  Our Lady of
      Copacabana

Borneo
  Francis Xavier

Brazil
  Our Lady of the
      Immaculate
      Conception
  Peter of Alcantara

Canada
  Anne
  Joseph
  Isaac Jogues
      and Companions

Central America
  Rose of Lima

Chile
  James the Greater
  Our Lady of
      Mt. Carmel

China
  Joseph

Colombia
  Peter Claver

Corsica
  Our Lady of
      the Immaculate
      Conception

William Luberoff. *Our Lady of Mt. Carmel (Contemporary)*

Costa Rica
  Our Lady of the Angels

Crete
  Titus

Cuba
  Our Lady of Charity

Cyprus
  Barnabas

Czech Republic
  John of Nepomucene

  Wenceslaus

Denmark
  Ansgar

  Canute

Dominican Republic
  Dominic

Dublin
  Kevin

Ecuador
  Most Pure Heart
    of Mary

Egypt
  Mark

El Salvador
  Our Lady of Peace

England
  George

  Augustine
    of Canterbury

Equatorial Guinea
  Our Lady of the
    Immaculate
    Conception

Ethiopia
  Frumentius

Robert Berran. *St. Dominic (Contemporary)*

Europe

Benedict of Nursia

Bridget of Sweden

Catherine of Siena

Cyril and Methodius

Finland

Henry of Uppsala

France

Louis IX

Martin of Tours

Joan of Arc

Our Lady of
the Assumption

Therese of Lisieux

Germany

Ansgar

Boniface

Michael

Peter Canisius

Gibraltar

Bernard of Clairvaux

Michael

Greece

Andrew

Nicholas of Myra

Paul

Haiti

Our Lady of
Perpetual Help

Holland

Willibrord

Honduras

Our Lady of Suyapa

Hungary

Elizabeth of Hungary

Stephen of Hungary

Robert Berran. *St. Joan of Arc (Contemporary)*

Iceland
Ansgar

India
Francis Xavier

Our Lady of
   the Assumption

Ireland
Bridget of Ireland

Columba

Patrick

Italy
Bernardine of Siena

Catherine of Siena

Francis of Assisi

Jamaica
Our Lady of the
   Assumption

Japan
Peter Baptist

Francis Xavier

Jordan
John the Baptist

Korea
Joseph and Mary

Lesotho
Immaculate Heart
   of Mary

Lithuania
Casimir of Poland

Cunegund

John of Kanty

Luxembourg
Cunegund

Willibrord

St. Catherine of Siena (Contemporary)

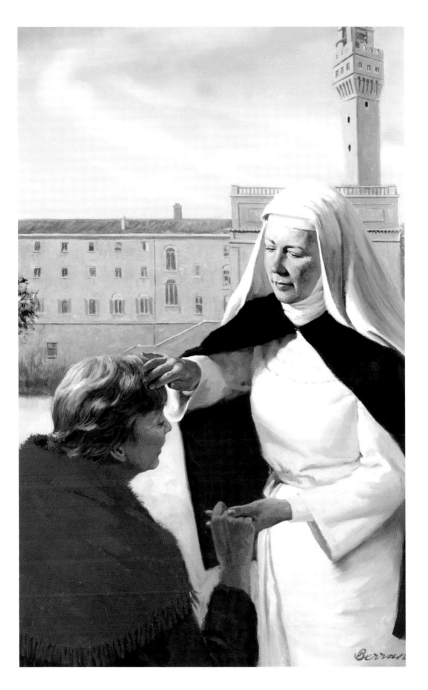

Madagascar
Vincent de Paul

Malta
Paul
Our Lady of
the Assumption

Mexico
Our Lady of
Guadalupe
Joseph

Monaco
Devota

Moravia
Cyril and Methodius
Wenceslaus

Naples
Januarius

New Zealand
Our Lady Help
of Christians

Nicaragua
James the Greater

Nigeria
Patrick

North Africa
Cyprian of Carthage

North America
Isaac Jogues
and Companions

Norway
Olaf

Oceana
Peter Chanel

Pakistan
Francis Xavier

Robert Berran. *St. Francis Xavier (Contemporary)*

Papua New Guinea

Michael

Paraguay

Our Lady of
the Assumption

Our Lady of Lujan

Peru

Joseph

Rose of Lima

Turibius of Mongrovejo

Philippines

Rose of Lima

Sacred Heart of Mary

Poland

Adalbert

Casimir of Poland

Cunegund

Florian

Stanislaus of Cracow

Stanislaus Kostka

Portugal

Anthony of Padua

Elizabeth of Portugal

Francis Borgia

George

Our Lady of the
Immaculate
Conception

Vincent of Saragossa

Puerto Rico

Our Lady of Divine
Providence

Rome

Philip Neri

Russia

Andrew

Basil the Great

Casimir of Poland

Therese of Lisieux

William Luberoff. *St. Rose of Lima (Contemporary)*

Sardinia
Maurice

Scandinavia
Ansgar

Scotland
Andrew

Columba

Margaret of Scotland

Sicily
Lucy

Nicholas of Myra

Vitus

Silesia
Hedwig

Slovakia
Wenceslaus

Solomon Islands
Michael

South Africa
Our Lady of
the Assumption

South America
Rose of Lima

Spain
James the Greater

John of Avila

Teresa of Avila

Sri Lanka
Lawrence

Sweden
Bridget of Sweden

Tanzania
Our Lady of the
Immaculate
Conception

Turkey
John the Apostle

William Luberoff. *Our Lady of the Assumption (Contemporary)*

United States
Our Lady of the
Immaculate
Conception

Uruguay
Blessed Virgin Mary

Philip and James

Venezuela
Our Lady
of Coromoto

Vietnam
Joseph

Wales
David of Wales

West Indies
Gertrude the Great

Rose of Lima

Yugoslavia
Cyril and Methodius

Zaire
Our Lady of the
Immaculate
Conception

Calendar of Saints' Feast Days

January

1   Solemnity of Mary, Mother of God
2   St. Basil, St. Gregory Nazianzen
4   St. Elizabeth Ann Seton
5   St. John Neumann
6   Blessed André Bessette
     The Epiphany of the Lord
         (or Sunday between January 2 and January 8)
7   St. Raymond of Peñafort
13   St. Hilary
17   St. Anthony
20   St. Fabian, St. Sebastian
21   St. Agnes
22   St. Vincent
24   St. Francis de Sales
25   Conversion of St. Paul
26   St. Timothy, St. Titus
27   St. Angela Merici
28   St. Thomas Aquinas
31   St. John Bosco
     The Baptism of the Lord
         (Sunday after January 6 or Sunday after the Epiphany of the Lord)

Berran.

February

2   Presentation of the Lord
3   St. Blaise, St. Ansgar
5   St. Agatha
6   St. Paul Miki and Companions
8   St. Jerome Emiliani
10 St. Scholastica
11 Our Lady of Lourdes
14 St. Cyril, St. Methodius
17 Seven Holy Founders of the
     Servite Order
21 St. Peter Damian
22 Chair of St. Peter
23 St. Polycarp

March

3   St. Katharine Drexel
4   St. Casimir
7   St. Perpetua, St. Felicity
8   St. John of God
9   St. Frances of Rome
17 St. Patrick

Robert Berran. *St. Patrick (Contemporary)*

18   St. Cyril of Jerusalem
19   St. Joseph, Spouse of the Virgin Mary
23   St. Turibius of Mogrovejo
25   The Annunciation of the Lord

April

2   St. Francis of Paola
4   St. Isidore
5   St. Vincent Ferrer
7   St. John Baptist de la Salle
11   St. Stanislaus
13   St. Martin I
21   St. Anselm
23   St. George
24   St. Fidelis of Sigmaringen
25   St. Mark
28   St. Peter Chanel
29   St. Catherine of Siena
30   St. Pius V

May

1   St. Joseph the Worker

2   St. Athanasius

3   Sts. Philip and James

12 St. Nereus, St. Achilleus, St. Pancras

14 St. Matthias

15 St. Isidore

18 St. John I

20 St. Bernardine of Siena

25 St. Bede the Venerable

     St. Gregory VII

     St. Mary Magdalene de Pazzi

26 St. Philip Neri

27 St. Augustine of Canterbury

31 Visitation of the Blessed Virgin Mary

     The Holy Trinity

        (First Sunday after Pentecost)

     The Body and Blood of Christ

        (Thursday or Sunday after Holy Trinity)

     The Sacred Heart of Jesus

        (Friday following Second Sunday after Pentecost)

     Immaculate Heart of Mary

        (Saturday following Second Sunday after Pentecost)

June

1   St. Justin

2   St. Marcellinus, St. Peter

3   Sts. Charles Lwanga and Companions

5   St. Boniface

6   St. Norbert

9   St. Ephrem of Syria

11   St. Barnabas

13   St. Anthony of Padua

19   St. Romuald

21   St. Aloysius Gonzaga

22   St. Paulinus of Nola, St. John Fisher,
       St. Thomas More

24   Birth of St. John the Baptist

27   St. Cyril of Alexandria

28   St. Irenaeus

29   Sts. Peter and Paul

30   First Martyrs of the Church of Rome

Robert Berran. *St. Anthony (Contemporary)*

July

1   Blessed Junipero Serra
3   St. Thomas
4   St. Elizabeth of Portugal
5   St. Athony Zaccaria
6   St. Maria Goretti
11 St. Benedict
13 St. Henry
14 Blessed Kateri Tekakwitha,
        St. Camillus de Lellis
15 St. Bonaventure
16 Our Lady of Mount Carmel
21 St. Lawrence of Brindisi
22 St. Mary Magdalene
23 St. Bridget of Sweden
25 St. James the Great
26 Sts. Joachim and Anne
29 St. Martha
30 St. Peter Chrysologus
31 St. Ignatius of Loyola

Robert Berran. *Blessed Kateri Tekakwitha (Contemporary)*

August

1   St. Alphonsus Liguori

2   St. Eusebius of Vercelli

4   St. John Vianney

5   Dedication of the Basilica of
       St. Mary Major

6   Transfiguration of the Lord

7   St. Sixtus II and Companions, St. Cajetan

8   St. Dominic

10   St. Lawrence

11   St. Claire

13   St. Pontian, St. Hippolytus

14   St. Maximilian Kolbe

15   Assumption of the Blessed Virgin Mary

16   St. Stephen of Hungary

19   St. John Eudes

20   St. Bernard

21   St. Pius X

22   Queenship of Mary

23   St. Rose of Lima

24   St. Bartholomew

25   St. Louis of France, St. Joseph Calasanz

27   St. Monica

28   St. Augustine of Hippo

29   Beheading of St. John the Baptist

September

3   St. Gregory the Great

8   Birth of the Blessed Virgin Mary

9   St. Peter Claver

13   St. John Chrysostom

14   The Holy Cross

15   Our Lady of Sorrows

16   Sts. Cyprian and Cornelius

17   St. Robert Bellarmine

19   St. Januarius

20   St. Andrew Kim Taegon, St. Paul Chong
      Hasang, and Companions

21   St. Matthew

26   Sts. Cosmas and Damian

27   St. Vincent de Paul

28   St. Wenceslaus, St. Lawrence Ruiz

29   Sts. Michael, Gabriel, and Raphael

30   St. Jerome

October

1   St. Therese of Lisieux

2   Guardian Angels

4   St. Francis of Assisi

6   St. Bruno, Blessed Marie Rose Durocher

7   Our Lady of the Rosary

9   St. Dennis and Companions,
      St. John Leonardi

14   St. Callistus

15   St. Teresa of Avila

16   St. Hedwig, St. Margaret Mary Alacoque

17   St. Ignatius of Antioch

18   St. Luke

19   Sts. Isaac Jogues,
      John de Brébeuf, and Companions,
      St. Paul of the Cross

23   St. John of Capistrano

24   St. Anthony Mary Claret

28   Sts. Simon and Jude

Robert Berran. *St. Teresa of Avila (Contemporary)*

November

1   All Saints

2   All Souls

3   St. Martin de Porres

4   St. Charles Borromeo

9   Dedication of St. John Lateran Basilica

10 St. Leo the Great

11 St. Martin of Tours

12 St. Josaphat

13 St. Frances Xavier Cabrini

15 St. Albert the Great

16 St. Margaret of Scotland,
     St. Gertrude the Great

17 St. Elizabeth of Hungary

18 Dedication of the Churches of St. Peter and
     St. Paul, St. Rose Philippine Duchesne

21 Presentation of the Virgin Mary

22 St. Cecilia

23 St. Clement, St. Columban,
     Blessed Miguel Augustin Pro

24 St. Andrew Dung-Lac and Companions

30 St. Andrew
     Christ the King (Last Sunday in ordinary time)

Robert Berran. *St. Frances Xavier Cabrini (Contemporary)*

December

3   St. Francis Xavier

4   St. John Damascene

6   St. Nicholas of Myra

7   St. Ambrose

8   Immaculate Conception of
      the Virgin Mary

9   St. Juan Diego

11 St. Damasus

12 Our Lady of Guadalupe,
      St. Jane Frances de Chantal

13 St. Lucy

14 St. John of the Cross

21 St. Peter Canisius

23 St. John of Kanty

26 St. Stephen

27 St. John, Apostle and Evangelist

28 Holy Innocents

29 St. Thomas Becket

31 St. Sylvester
     The Holy Family

       (Sunday within the octave of the Birth of the Lord
       or, if there is no Sunday within the octave, December 30)

Patron Saints Listing

Adalbert
Bohemia, Poland

Adjutor
yachtsmen

Adelaide
empresses, princesses, prisoners, second marriages

Adrian
soldiers

Agatha
firefighters, nurses, single laywomen, torture victims

Agnes
girls

Alban
refugees

Albert the Great
medical technicians, scientists, theological students

Alodia
runaways

Aloysius Gonzaga
students in Jesuit colleges and universities, youth

Alphais
disabled people

Alphonsus Liguori
confessors, religious vocations, theologians

Amand
hoteliers, wine trade

Ambrose
bee keepers, bishops, chandlers, learning

Anastasius
goldsmiths

Andrew
fishermen, gout
sufferers, Greece, sailors,
single women,
Russia, Scotland

Andronicus
silversmiths

Ansgar
Denmark,
Germany, Iceland,
Scandinavia,

Anne
cabinet makers,
Canada, childless
women, cemetaries,
expectant mothers,
grandmothers, horse
riders, homemakers,
mothers, widows,
women in labor

Anthony Claret
savings banks

Anthony of Egypt
amputees, basket
weavers, butchers,
domestic animals,
hermits, gravediggers,
monks, skin diseases,

Anthony of Padua
lost articles, Portugal,
skin rashes, the poor,
travelers

Apollonia
dentists, toothaches

Arthelais
kidnap victims

Augustine of Hippo
brewers, printers,
theologians

Augustine of Canterbury
England

Robert Berran. *St. Augustine (Contemporary)*

96

Barbara
ammunition workers, architects, builders, founders, brass workers, fireworks, miners, fortifications, gunners, impenitence, prisoners, stone masons, those in danger of sudden death by lightning and other means, storms, warehouses

Barnabas
Cyprus

Bartholomew
Armenia, tanners, plasterers

Basil the Great
hospital administrators, Russia

Bede the Venerable
scholars

Benedict
Europe, farm workers, death and dying, poison sufferers, speleologists

Benedict the Black
foriegn missions

Benedict Labre
homeless, mentally ill, tramps

Bernadette
sheepherders

Bernard of Clairvaux
Gibraltar

Bernard of Montjoux
alpinists, mountaineers, skiers

Bernardine of Siena
advertisers, communications, Italy, personnel, preachers, public relations, weavers

Robert Berran. *St. Benedict (Contemporary)*

Blaise
throat diseases

Blessed Virgin Mary
Korea, mothers, virgins,
Uruguay

Brendan
navigators, sailors,
whales

Boniface
Germany

Boris and Gleb
princes

Bridget of Ireland
dairy workers,
Ireland, scholars

Bridget of Sweden
Europe, nuns, Sweden

Bruno
the possessed

Bueno
sick children

Camillus de Lellis
hospitals, nurses,
sickness

Canute
Denmark

Casimir of Poland
bachelors, kings,
Lithuania, Poland,
princes, Russia

Castorius
sculptors

Cassian
stenographers

Catherine of Alexandria
students, throats

Catherine of Bologna
art, artists

Catherine of Genoa
victims of
unfaithfulness,
widows

Catherine of Siena
fire protection,
Europe, Italy,
nursing services,

Cecilia
composers, musicians,
organ builders, poets,
singers

Charles Borromeo
apple orchards, bishops,
catechists, colic
sufferers, priests,
seminarians, spiritual
directors, stomach
trouble, ulcers

**Charles Lwanga
and Companions**
African Catholic
youth, victims of torture

Charles the Good
courts, crusaders

Christopher
bachelors, bus drivers,
travelers, motorists,
pilgrims, porters, sailors,
truck drivers,

Claire of Assisi
childbirth,
diseases of the eye,
embroiderers,
television

Claude La Colombiere
sculptors

Clement of Alexandria
lighthouse keepers

Clement of Rome
marble workers,
stonecutters

Columba
Ireland, Scotland

Cosmas and Damian
confectioners, chemical industries, barbers, dentists, hairdressers, nurses, pharmacists, physicians, surgeons

Crispin and Crispinian
leatherworkers, saddlers, shoemakers, tanners

Cunegund
Lithuania, Luxembourg, Poland

Cuthbert
sailors, shepherders

Cuthman
sheepherders

Cyprian of Carthage
Algeria, North Africa

Cyril and Methodius
Bohemia, ecumenists, Europe, Moravia,

Damasus I
archaeologists

David of Wales
Wales

Dennis
headaches, the possessed

Devota
Monaco

Dismas
funeral directors, repentant thieves

Dominic
astronomers, Dominican Republic

Dominic Savio
choirboys, falsely accused, young boys

Dorothy
florists, gardeners

Drogo
mentally ill, sheepherders

Dunstan
armorers, goldsmiths, jewelers, locksmiths, musicians

Dymphna
epilepsy, family harmony, mental illness, princesses, runaways, sleepwalkers

Edgar
kings, widowers

Edmund
kings, victims of torture

Edward the Confessor
difficult marriages, kings, separated spouses

Edwin
homeless, kings

Eligius (Eloi)
coin collectors, goldsmiths, jewelers, locksmiths, metal workers

Elizabeth Ann Seton
widows

Elizabeth of Hungary
bakers, Catholic charities, countesses, nurses, death of children, falsely accused, homeless, Hungary, nursing services, nursing homes, victims of jealousy, widows

Elizabeth of Portugal
difficult marriages, Portugal, queens, victims of unfaithfulness

Erasmus
stomach disorders

Eustace
hunters

Fabiola
difficult marriages,
divorced, domestic
abuse victims,
victims of unfaithfulness

Felicity
barren women,
death of children,
widows

Ferdinand of Castile
engineers, governors

Fiacre
gardeners, taxi drivers

Flora
abandoned people

Florian
Austria, firemen,
Poland

Fra Angelico
artists

Frances of Rome
motorists, widows

Frances Xavier Cabrini
hospital administrators,
emigrants, orphans

Francis of Assisi
animals, Catholic action,
ecologists, fire, Italy,
merchants,
needleworkers,
solitary death

Francis Borgia
Portugal

Francis of Paola
mariners, navigators

Francis de Sales
confessors, journalists,
the Catholic press,
the hearing impaired,
teachers, writers

Robert Berran. *St. Francis de Sales (Contemporary)*

Francis Xavier
apostleship of prayer,
Borneo, foreign
missions, India, Japan,
Pakistan, wine trade

Frumentius
Ethiopia

Gabriel
Argentina, diplomats,
messengers, postal
employees, radio and
telecommunications,
television workers

Gabriel Possenti
priests, youth

Gemma Galgani
pharmacists,
tuberculosis

Genesius
actors, comedians,
dancers, epilepsy,
lawyers, secretaries,
stenographers,
printers, organ builders

Genevieve
fever patients,
servicewomen

George
archers, Boy Scouts,
calvary, chivalry,
England, farmers,
knights, soldiers,
skin rashes, Portugal

Gerald of Aurillac
disabled people

Gerard Majella
childbirth, expectant
mothers, lay brothers,
mothers

Germaine Cousin
sheepherders, the sick

Gertrude the Great
West Indies

Gilbert of Sempringham
crippled people

Robert Berran. *St. Gertrude (Contemporary)*

Giles
  crippled people,
  hermits, horses, lepers,

Goar
  potters

Godaleva
  domestic abuse, victims

Gotteschalc
  linguists, lost vocations,
  princes

Gregory the Illuminator
  Armenia

Gregory of Neocaesarea
  desperate cases

Gregory the Great
  musicians, popes,
  singers, students,
  teachers

Guntramnus
  divorced, guardians

Hedwig
  duchesses, Silesia,
  victims of jealousy,
  queens

Helen
  archaeologists,
  converts, difficult
  marriages, empresses,
  the divorced

Henry of Uppsala
  Finland

Henry II
  disabled people, dukes

Hippolitus
  horses

Holy Innocents
  choir boys, foundlings

Homobonus
  clothworkers,
  merchants, tailors

Hubert
dogs, hunters, machinists, mathematicians, victims of rabies

Ignatius of Loyola
retreats, soldiers

Immaculate Heart of Mary
Angola, Lesotho

Isaac Jogues and Companions
Canada, North America

Isidore the Farmer
farmers, laborers

Isidore of Seville
internet

Ives
advocates, judges, lawyers

James the Greater
arborers, arthritis,

Chili, knights, Nicaragua, pilgrims, pharmacists, Spain

James the Less
hatters

Januarius
blood banks, Naples, volcanoes

Jason
converts

Jerome
archaeologists, librarians, scholars,

Jerome Emiliani
orphans

Joan of Arc
France, soldiers, servicewomen,

John the Apostle
Asia Minor, blood banks, booksellers, compositors,

engravers, paper
makers, publishers,
theologians, Turkey,
writers

John of Avila
Spain

John of God
alcoholics,
booksellers, heart
patients, hospitals,
nurses, printers, the sick

John the Baptist
Jordan, monks, tailors

John Baptist de la Salle
teachers

John Berchmans
altar servers, youth

John Bosco
editors, laborers,
publishers, young
apprentices, youth

John Capistrano
jurists

John Chrysostom
jurists, orators,
preachers

John Gualbert
forest workers

John of Kanty
Lithuania

John of the Cross
mystics

John of Nepomucene
Belgium, Bohemia,
bridges, confessors,
Czech Republic,
those who have been
slandered

John Neumann
Catholic education

John Roche
boatmen

Robert Berran. *St. John Bosco (Contemporary)*

John Vianney
  priests

Josephat
  ecumenists

Joseph
  Austria, Belgium,
  Bohemia, Canada,
  China, carpenters,
  doubters, dying,
  engineers, families,
  fathers, guardians,
  hesitators, laborers,
  Korea,, Mexico,
  Peru, pioneers, social
  justice, spouses,
  the Church, tramps,
  universal church,
  Vietnam

Joseph Cafasso
  prisons

Joseph Calasanz
  Catholic schools

Joseph of Arimathea
  funeral directors,
  pall bearers

Joseph of Cupertino
  astronauts, aviators, air
  passengers, pilots,
  students

Jude Thaddeus
  desperate causes,
  hospital workers

Julian the Hospitaler
  boatmen, knights

Kevin
  Dublin, long life

Killian
  Bavaria

Lawrence
  cooks, deacons,
  firefighters,
  the poor,
  Sri Lanka

Justin Martyr
  philosophers

Lambert
  children

Leonard of Port Maurice
  parish missions

Leopold
  Austria, Lidwina,
  skaters, stepparents

Louis IX
  Crusaders, France,
  grooms, kings,
  prisoners, sickness,

Louise de Marillac
  social workers

Lucian and Marcian
  the possessed

Lucy
  cutters, eye diseases,
  writers, the blind,
  peasants, saddlers,
  salepeople, Sicily

Luke
  artists, brewers,
  jewelers, glassworkers,
  glaziers, goldsmiths,
  painters, physicians,
  sculptors, surgeons,
  notaries, nursing homes

Lydia
  dyers

Magnus
  fishmarkets

Margaret of Contona
  homeless, midwives,
  single mothers, single
  women

Margaret of Fontana
  the possessed

Margaret of Scotland
  death and dying,
  widows, Scotland

Margaret of York
  business women

Maria Goretti
girls

Marinus
deacons

Mark
Egypt, glassworkers, opticians, notaries, nursing homes, secretaries

Martha
cooks, dieticians, homemakers, hoteliers, innkeepers, lay sisters, restaurants, servants, waiters

Martin de Porres
African Americans, barbers, hairdressers, public education, public health service, race relations, social justice, the poor, the sick

Martin of Tours
beggars, France, soldiers

Mary Magdalene
hairdressers, penitents

Mary, Queen of Africa
Africa

Matilda
second marriages, widows

Matthew
accountants, alcoholics, bankers, bookkeepers, stockbrokers, tax collectors

Matthias
carpenters

Maurice
Austria, dyers, infantrymen, Sardinia, swordsmiths, weavers

Maurus
coppersmiths

Maximilian Kolbe
drug addicts and
their families

Michael
battle, Germany,
Gibraltor, grocers,
mariners,
Papua New Guinea,
paratroopers, police,
sickness, radiologists,
temptation,
Solomon Islands

Monica
alcoholics, difficult
marriages, mothers,
victims of abuse, widows

Most Pure Heart of Mary
Ecuador

Nicholas of Flue
councilmen, magistrates

Nicholas of Myra
apothecaries, bakers,
brides, brewers,
children, fishermen,
Greece, grooms,
merchants,
pawnbrokers,
perfumers, pharmacists,
sailors, Sicily, travelers

Nicholas of Tolentino
mothers, poor souls

Norbert
Bohemia

Notburga
field workers

Odilia
Alsace, blindness

Olaf
kings, Norway

Osmund
paralyzed people,
toothaches

Our Lady of the Assumption
France, India, Malta, Paraguay, South Africa

Our Lady of Copacabana
Bolivia

Our Lady of Charity
Cuba

Our Lady of Divine Providence
Puerto Rico

Our Lady of Grace
motorcyclists

Our Lady of Guadalupe
Americas, Mexico

Our Lady of Help Christians
Australia, Mexico

Our Lady of the Immaculate Conception
Corsica, Brazil,

Equatorial, Guinea, Portugal

Our Lady of Good Counsel
enlightenment

Our Lady of Loretto
aviators, air passengers, home builders, lace makers

Our Lady of Lourdes
bodily ills

Our Lady of Lujan
Argentina, Paraguay

Our Lady of the Miraculous Medal
motorcyclists

Our Lady of Mount Carmel
Chili

Our Lady of Peace
El Salvador

William Luberoff. *Our Lady of Guadalupe (Contemporary)*

Our Lady of Perpetual Help
never failing hope, Haiti

Our Lady of the Angels
Costa Rica

Our Lady of Suyapa
Honduras

Our Lady Who Appeared
Brazil

Paschal Baylon
Eucharistic congresses and societies

Patrick
Ireland, Nigeria, snakebite sufferers, toothache sufferers

Paul
Cursillo, Greece, Malta, public relations, publishers, rope makers, snakebites sufferers, toothaches, travelers writers

Paula
widows

Peregrine
cancer patients, skin disease sufferers

Perpetua
cows

Peter Canisius
Germany

Peter Chanel
Oceania

Peter Claver
Colombia, foreign missions, race relations

Peter
bridge builders, clock makers, fever patients, foot trouble, frenzy, fishermen, long life, net makers, popes, stationers, ship builders, the Church, wolves

William Luberoff. *St. Peter (Contemporary)*

Peter of Alcantara
  Brazil, watchmen

Peter Baptist
  Japan

Pharaildis
  abuse victims

Philemon
  dancers

Philip and James
  Uruguay

Philip Neri
  Rome

Phocas
  agricultural workers

Pollio
  lectors

Polycarp
  earache sufferers

Raphael
  blindness, eye diseases,
  happy meetings, lovers,
  nurses, pharmacists,
  physicians, travelers,
  sheepherders

Raymond Nonnatus
  midwives, obstetricians,
  those falsely accused,

Raymond of Peñafort
  canon lawyers,
  librarians

Rene Goupil
  anesthetists

Richard of Chichester
  coachmen

Rita of Cascia
  desperate situations,
  healing wounds, lonely
  people, tumors,
  unhappily married
  women

Robert Berran. *St. Rita (Contemporary)*

Robert Bellarmine
  catechists

Roch
  bachelors, dog lovers,
  invalids, plague
  victims

Rose of Lima
  Central America,
  florists,
  South America,
  Peru, the Americas, the
  Philippines, the West
  Indies, vanity

Sabas
  lectors

Sacred Heart of Mary
  Philippines

Scholastica
  convulsive children,
  nuns

Sebastian
  archers, athletes,
  cattle diseases, enemies

of religion, funeral
directos, hardware, lace
makers, plague victims,
physicians, potters,
racquet makers,
soldiers, stone
masons, swans

Seraphina
  disabled people,
  spinners

Servulus
  disabled people

Simon of Trent
  kidnap victims

Stanislaus of Cracow
  Poland

Stanislaus Kostka
  Poland

Star of the Sea
  mariners, navigators

Stephen
  bricklayers, casket

makers, deacons,
death of children,
headache sufferers,
stone masons

Stephen of Hungary
death of children,
kings, Hungary

Tarcisius
first communicants

Terese of Avila
headaches, heart
patients, Spain,

Theobald
church sextons, janitors

Therese of Lisieux
aviators, florists,
foreign missions,
France, Russia

Thomas the Apostle
architects, blindness,
carpenters, construction
workers

Thomas Aquinas
Catholic schools,
chastity, pencil
makers, students,
scholars, Theologians
universities

Thomas More
adopted children,
civil servants, difficult
marriages, lawyers,
stepparents, widowers

Timothy
stomach trouble

Titus
Crete

Turibius of Mongrovejo
Peru

Valentine
greetings, lovers

Viator
catechists

Vincent de Paul
  charitable organizations,
  hospital workers, lepers,
  Madagascar, prisoners,
  spiritual help

Vincent Ferrer
  builders, plumbers

Vincent Pallotti
  missionary priests,
  priests

Vincent of Saragossa
  Portugal, wine trade

Vitus
  comedians, dancers,
  epilepsy, those with
  dog and snake bites,
  Sicily

Vladimir
  converts, parents of
  large families,
  murderers

Walstan
  agricultural workers

Wenceslaus
  Bohemia, Czech
  Republic, Moravia,
  Slovakia

William
  adopted children

Willibrord
  epilepsy,
  Holland,
  Luxembourg

Zita
  homemakers, maids,
  servants

Robert Berran. *St. Vincent de Paul (Contemporary)*

Prayer to My Patron Saint

You lived a blessed life devoted to making the world a more divine place. Help me see the truth of God's teachings with every breath I take. Share with me your wisdom, compassion, and love of all things good. Give me courage to follow the way of Christ and never lose my belief in the power of His miracles. Guide my steps so they lead directly to God, and use your heavenly influence to keep me in God's goodness and mercy until the day we meet in Paradise. I give myself into your care. Amen.

Bibliography

Broderick, Robert C. *The Catholic Encyclopedia*, Thomas Nelson Publishers, Nashville, TN, 1976 "

Clifford, Diarmuid, O.P., *Patron Saints*, Saint Martin Apostolate, Dublin, Ireland, 1995.

Freze Michael, S.F.O. *Our Patron Saints*, Our Sunday Visitor, Inc., Huntington, IN, 1992.

McBrien, Richard P., *Lives of the Saints*, Harper San Francisco, A Division of HarperCollins Publishers, New York, N.Y. 2001.